Orthodox
Prayer Book

Orthodox Prayer Book
ISBN 979-8-9886216-4-5
Copyright © 2025 Eugen V. Rosu
Capricorn Publishing
www.capricornpublishing.space

Table of Contents

MORNING PRAYERS	1
PRAYERS FOR FAMILY	12
PRAYERS FOR MEALS	14
EVENING PRAYERS	16
PRAYERS FOR VARIOUS NEEDS	27
PREPARATION FOR HOLY COMMUNION	34
PRAYERS OF THANKSGIVING	50

MORNING PRAYERS

Glory to you, O God, Glory to you.

Prepare yourself in stillness and with thanksgiving in your heart, then make the sign of the cross and begin:

Through the prayers of our holy fathers, O Lord Jesus Christ our God, have mercy on us and save us. Amen.

Glory to you, O God, glory to you.

Heavenly King, Comforter, Spirit of truth, who are present everywhere and fulfilling all things; Treasury of blessings and Source of life, come abide in us, cleanse us of all stain, and save our souls, O Good One.

Holy God, Holy Mighty, Holy Immortal, have mercy on us. Holy God, Holy Mighty, Holy Immortal, have mercy on us. Holy God, Holy Mighty, Holy Immortal, have mercy on us.

Glory to the Father and to the Son and to the Holy Spirit, Now and ever and unto ages of ages. Amen.

All holy Trinity, have mercy on us. Lord, cleanse us of our sins. Master, forgive our transgressions. Holy One, look down on us and heal our infirmities to the glory of your name.

Lord, have mercy. Lord, have mercy. Lord, have mercy.

Glory to the Father and to the Son and to the Holy Spirit,

Now and ever and unto ages of ages. Amen.

Our Father who are in heaven, hallowed be your name. Your kingdom come, your will be done on earth as it is in heaven. Give us this day our daily bread and forgive us our trespasses as we forgive those who trespass against us. And lead us not into temptation but deliver us from the evil one.

Through the prayers of our holy fathers, O Lord Jesus Christ our God, have mercy on us and save us. Amen.

And then the following prayers:

Arising from sleep, we fall down before you, O Good One, and cry out the words of the angelic hymn, O Almighty: Holy, holy, holy are you, O God. Through the prayers of your angels have mercy on us.

Glory to the Father and to the Son and to the Holy Spirit.

You have raised me from bed and from sleep, O Lord; illumine my mind and open my heart and lips that I may praise you, O God. Through the prayers of all your saints, have mercy on us.

Now and ever and unto ages of ages. Amen.
The Judge will come unexpectedly, and everyone's deeds will be revealed. Thus, we cry fearfully at midnight: Holy, holy, holy are you, O God. Through the Birthgiver of God have mercy on us.

Lord, have mercy. *(12 times)*

Arising from sleep, I thank you, O all holy Trinity, for in your great goodness and long-suffering patience you have not turned your anger upon me, a lazy sinner, nor have you let me perish in my transgressions, but have dealt with me according to your love for mankind. You have lifted me from my despair, that I may be vigilant and glorify your might. Now, therefore, illumine the eyes of my mind and open my mouth that I may learn your words, understand your precepts and do your will, and thus I will sing to you wholeheartedly and praise your all holy name of the Father and of the Son and of the Holy Spirit, now and ever and unto ages of ages. Amen.

Glory to you, O King, almighty God, who in your divine care and love for mankind have granted me, a worthless sinner, to arise from sleep and enter your holy house. O Lord, also accept the voice of my prayers like those of your all holy and wise angelic powers, and grant that with purity of heart and meekness of spirit I may bring you praise from my soiled lips. With the torch of my soul thus illuminated may I also be numbered among the wise virgins and extol you, God the Word, glorified in the Father and the Spirit. Amen.

Come, let us worship God our King. Come, let us worship and bow down before Christ our King. Come, let us worship and bow down before Christ himself, our God and King.

Psalm 51

Have mercy on me, O God, in your goodness, in your great tenderness wipe away my faults; wash me clean of my guilt, purify me from my sin. For I am well aware of my faults, I have my sin constantly in mind, having sinned against none other than you, having done what you regard as wrong. You are just when you pass sentence on me, blameless when you give judgment. You know I was born guilty, a sinner from the moment of conception. Yet, since you love sincerity of heart, teach me the secrets of wisdom. Purify me with hyssop until I am clean; wash me until I am whiter than snow. Instill some joy and gladness into me, let the bones you have crushed rejoice again. Hide your face from my sins, wipe out all my guilt. God, create a clean heart in me, put into me a new and constant spirit, do not banish me from your presence, do not deprive me of your Holy Spirit. Be my savior again, renew my joy, keep my spirit steady and willing; and I shall teach transgressors the way to you, and to you the sinners will return. Save me from death, God my savior, and my tongue will acclaim your righteousness; Lord, open my lips and my mouth will speak out your praise. Sacrifice gives you no pleasure, were I to offer holocaust, you would not have it. My sacrifice is this broken spirit, you will not scorn this crushed and broken heart. Show your favor graciously to Zion, rebuild the walls of Jerusalem. Then there will be proper sacrifice to please you -- and young bulls to be offered on your altar.

First Prayer

By St. Macarius

O Lord, cleanse me a sinner, for I have never done anything good in your sight; deliver me from the evil one and let your will be in me so that I may open my unworthy mouth without condemnation and praise your holy name of the Father and of the Son and of the Holy Spirit, now and ever unto ages of ages. Amen.

Second Prayer

By St. Macarius

Arising from sleep, I bring the midnight song to you, O Savior, and falling before you I cry out: Do not let me sleep the death of sinners, but have mercy on me as I lie in lethargy, O Hasten, raise me up and save me, for I stand before you in prayer. After the sleep of night, illumine this day without sin, O Lord Christ and save me.

Third Prayer

By St. Macarius

Arising from sleep I flee to you, O Master, lover of mankind, and strive to do works pleasing to you. I pray to you, in your compassion always help me and in all things. Deliver me from all evil worldly works and save me from all diabolic attacks, leading me into your eternal kingdom. For you are my creator, protector, and bestower of all good things, and all my hope is in you, and I glorify you now and ever and unto ages of ages. Amen.

Fourth Prayer

By St. Macarius

O Lord, in your great goodness and abundant compassion, you have granted me, your servant, to pass the time of this night without falling into any of the evil temptations of the jealous enemy. O Master and Creator of all, by your true light, grant that with an illumined heart I may do your will now and ever and unto ages of ages. Amen.

Fifth Prayer

By St. Macarius

O Lord, almighty God, who accept the thrice-holy hymn from the heavenly powers, receive also from us, your unworthy servants, the song of Holy! Holy! Holy! In every year and hour of our lives enable us to send up glory to you; to the Father and to the Son and to the Holy Spirit, now and ever and unto ages of ages. Amen.

Sixth Prayer

By St. Basil the Great

O almighty Lord, God of the powers and of all flesh, who dwell in the heights and care for those on earth, who search the hearts and depths of men and who truly know all our hidden thoughts; ever-living Light from all eternity, in whom there is neither change, nor shadow, nor alteration: Accept our prayers which we offer from stained lips at this hour of the night, O immortal King. As we place our hope in your abundant mercy, forgive every sin which we have committed against you in word or deed, in knowledge or in ignorance. Cleanse us of all stain of body or soul and make us the honored temple of your Holy Spirit. Grant that with a pure and wakeful heart we may pass the night of this life in anticipation of the brilliant and holy day when your only-begotten Son, our Lord, God and Savior, Jesus Christ, will come with glory upon earth to judge and render to each according to his deeds. May we not be found idle or sleeping, but watchful and wakefully performing your commandments. May we be prepared to enter into his divine and glorious bridal chamber where the voice of those who praise you is unceasing and the sweetness of those who behold the ineffable beauty of your glory is indescribable. For you are the true Light who enlightens and sanctifies all, and all creation glorifies you forever. Amen.

Seventh Prayer

By St. Basil

We bless you, O most-high God and Lord of mercies who ever work great, indescribable, glorious, and numerous deeds for us. You have granted us sleep so that we may rest from our weakness, and as repose from our physical efforts. We thank you for not abandoning us to our transgressions, but rather you have shown your customary love for mankind and lifted us up so that we may hasten to glorify your power. Therefore we beseech your abundant goodness: Enlighten the eyes of our hearts, raise our minds from the burdensome sleep of indolence, open our mouths and fill them with your praise, so that in all tranquility we may sing, cry out, and ever confess you: God, who are glorified in all and by all; the Father who is without beginning, together with your only-begotten Son and your all holy, good and life-giving Spirit, now and ever and unto ages of ages. Amen.

Eighth Prayer

By St. John Chrysostom

Lord, do not deprive me of your heavenly blessings. Lord, deliver me from eternal torments. Lord, if I have sinned in mind, in thought, in word, or in deed, forgive me. Lord, deliver me from all ignorance, forgetfulness, cowardice, and hard indifference. Lord, deliver me from all temptation. Lord, enlighten my heart which has been darkened by lust. Lord, I, being , mortal, have sinned; look upon my feeble soul, for you are a God of compassion, and have mercy on me. Lord, send your mercy to help me so that I may extol your glorious name. Lord, Jesus Christ, inscribe me, your servant, in the book of life, and grant that the end of my life may be peaceful. Lord, though I have done nothing good in your sight, grant that through your grace I may now make a good beginning, Lord, shower the dew of your grace upon my heart. Lord of heaven and earth, remember me, your sinful, shameful, and unclean servant, in your Kingdom. Amen.

Lord, accept me in penitence. Lord, do not leave me. Lord, do not lead me into temptation. Lord, grant me good thoughts. Lord, grant me tears, remembrance of death, and humility. Lord, grant me the thought of confessing all my sins, Lord, grant me humility, chastity, and obedience. Lord, grant me patience, courage, and meekness. Lord, implant in me the root of blessings and the fear of you in my heart. Lord, grant that I may love you with all my mind and soul and that I may do your will in all things. Lord, deliver me from contentious men, from the devil, from bodily passions and from all unholy deeds. I know, O Lord, that you act according to your will; may your will also be in me, a sinner, for you are blessed unto all ages. Amen.

Ninth Prayer

To the Guardian Angel

I fall before you, my holy guardian, angel of Christ, for you were given to me at holy baptism to guard my soul and my sinful body. Through my indolence and bad habits I have angered your pure light and driven you from me by my shameful ways: by lies, slander, jealousy, judgment, pride, stubbornness, lack of love for my brothers, and remembering evils, by love of money, worldly pleasures, anger, extravagance, food and drink beyond measure, by excessive talking, evil thoughts, bad habits, and lust for passions. Even the dumb beasts do not have the evil inclinations which are in me. How can you bear to look at me, or how can you draw near to me who am so defiled? O angel of Christ, with what eyes will you look upon me who am entangled in stained deeds? How can I beg forgiveness for all my bitter, evil, and wicked sins which I commit each day. Each night, and at every hour? Therefore, I fall before you and pray: O my holy Guardian, have compassion on me, a sinner; be my helper and supporter against the evil one, and by your holy intercessions make me a participant of the kingdom of God together with all the saints, now and ever and unto ages of ages. Amen.

Tenth Prayer

To the Birthgiver of God

O my most holy Lady, Birthgiver of God, banish from me, your lowly and sinful servant, despair, forgetfulness, ignorance, negligence, and all impure, evil and blasphemous thoughts from my wretched heart and my darkened mind. Quench the flame of my passions, for I am poor and miserable. Keep me from the remembrance of all troublesome thoughts and passions and free me from all evil deeds. For you are blessed by all generations and your all glorious name is extolled unto all ages. Amen.

Prayer

By Metropolitan Philaret of Moscow

O Lord, grant that I may greet the coming day in peace. Help me to rely upon your holy will at every moment. In every hour of the day, reveal your will to me. Bless my association with all who surround me. Teach me to treat whatever may happen to me throughout the day with peace of soul and with firm conviction that your will governs all. In all my deeds and words, guide my thoughts and feelings. In unforeseen events, let me not forget that all are sent by you. Teach me to act firmly and wisely, without embittering and embarrassing others. Give me strength to bear the fatigue of the coming day with all that it shall bring. Direct my will. Teach me to pray. Pray yourself in me. Amen.

Final Prayer

To the Birthgiver of God

O my gracious Queen, my hope, Birthgiver of God, who receive the poor and help the travelers; joy of those who sorrow, shelter for the oppressed: Behold my affliction and see my needs. Help me as you would one in despair; feed me as you would a stranger. You know all my troubles, absolve them according to your will, for I have no other help but you, no other ready shelter or comfort but you, O mother of God, to help me and protect me unto ages of ages. Amen.

It is truly right to call you blessed, O Birthgiver of God; ever-blessed and most pure, and Mother of our God. More honorable than the cherubim, and more glorious beyond compare than the seraphim, who without loss of virginity gave birth to God the Word. True Birthgiver of God, we praise you.

Glory to the Father and to the Son and to the Holy Spirit, now and ever and unto ages of ages. Amen.

Lord, have mercy. Lord, have mercy. Lord, have mercy.

Through the prayers of our holy fathers, O Lord Jesus Christ, our God, have mercy on us and save us. Amen.

PRAYERS FOR FAMILY

Parents' Prayer For Their Children

Lord our God, who in your wisdom created man from the earth and breathed the breath of life into him, blessing him and saying: Be fruitful and multiply, and fill the earth; and at Cana of Galilee, through your Only-begotten Son, you blessed the wedding, and thus also blessed the birth of children. In humility I call upon your goodness, asking that you unceasingly pour out your grace and have blessed me with. Fill them with wisdom and understanding. Protect them from all the visible and invisible snares of the evil one. Command your angels to ever be with them and guide them toward good works, so that they may always praise and glorify you all the days of their lives. Amen.

Prayer For Husbands and Wives

Lord, Jesus Christ our God, who taught us to pray continually for one another, thus fulfilling your commandment and manifesting our desire for your mercy, in your compassion, watch over and protect my husband (wife) from all seen and unseen enemies. Grant him (her) health and complete wisdom so that he (she) may fulfill all his (her) obligations according to your will and commandments. Protect him (her) from all temptations which he (she) does not have the strength to resist. Strengthen him (her) in the right faith and in perfect love, that we may live together in virtue, and direct our lives according to your precepts. For yours is the power and glory for ever. Amen.

We implore you, O merciful Lord: Help us to remember that marriage is indeed holy, and strengthen the sanctity of our union. Shower your grace upon us so that we may live our lives in true faithfulness and love. Help us to understand and trust each other fully, keeping quarrels and arguments far from us. Bestow your blessings upon us, and in your mercy, count us worthy of your kingdom: for you are our sanctification, and we offer glory to you: to the Father and to the Son and to the Holy Spirit, now and ever and unto ages and ages. Amen.

Prayer For Your Parents

O God of goodness, who have given me parents through whom I may partake of your many blessings; whose desire it is that I give thanks for the life which you have given me through them and for the care which they have shown me; I humbly pray to you for their health and salvation. Long-suffering, gracious and righteous God, accept my humble thanks for the blessings which you have unceasingly poured out upon my parents. Good Master, continue to send your grace upon them and forgive all in which they have sinned and in which, as mortals, they will err in the future. In your goodness, reward them for the love and care which they have constantly shown me; protect them from all accidents and sadness; give them a long, peaceful and happy life. May your blessings flow upon us all and grant that we may do all those things which please you, so that together we may bless you all the days of our lives. Amen.

PRAYERS FOR MEALS

Before Breakfast or Lunch

In the name of the Father and of the Son and of the Holy Spirit.

Our Father who are in heaven, hallowed be your name. Your kingdom come, your will be done on earth as it is in heaven. Give us this day our daily bread, and forgive us our trespasses as we forgive those who trespass against us. And lead us not into temptation, but deliver us from the evil one.

Glory to the Father and to the Son and to the Holy Spirit, now and ever and unto ages of ages.

Amen.

Lord, have mercy. Lord, have mercy. Lord, have mercy.

Through the prayers of our holy fathers, O Lord Jesus Christ our God, have mercy on us and save us. Amen.

After Breakfast or Lunch

We thank you, Christ our God, for you have satisfied us with your earthly gifts. Grant that we may not be unworthy of your heavenly kingdom; but as you were present among your disciples, O Savior, giving them peace, come also among us and save us. Amen.

Glory to the Father and to the Son and to the Holy Spirit,

now and ever and unto ages of ages. Amen.

Lord, have mercy. Lord, have mercy. Lord, have mercy.

Through the prayers of our holy fathers, O Lord Jesus Christ our God, have mercy on us and save us. Amen.

Before Supper

The poor shall eat and be satisfied and those who seek the Lord will praise him; their hearts shall live forever.

Glory to the Father and to the Son and to the Holy Spirit, now and ever and unto ages of ages. Amen.

Lord, have mercy. Lord, have mercy. Lord, have mercy.

Through the prayers of our holy fathers, O Lord Jesus Christ our God, have mercy on us and save us. Amen.

After Supper

Lord, let the light of your face shine upon us. You have given more joy to my heart than others ever knew for all their corn and wine. In peace I lie down and fall asleep at once, since you alone, Lord, make me rest secure.

Glory to the Father and to the Son and to the Holy Spirit, now and ever and unto ages of ages. Amen.

Lord, have mercy. Lord, have mercy. Lord, have mercy.

Evening Prayers

Through the prayers of our holy fathers, O Lord Jesus Christ our God, have mercy on us and save us. Amen.

Glory to you, O God, glory to you.

Heavenly King, Comforter, Spirit of truth, who are present everywhere and fulfilling all things; Treasury of blessings and Source of life, come abide in us, cleanse us of all stain, and save our souls, O Good One.

Holy God, Holy Mighty, Holy Immortal, have mercy on us. Holy Mighty, Holy Immortal, have mercy on us. Holy God, Holy Mighty, Holy Immortal, have mercy on us.

Glory to the Father and to the Son and to the Holy Spirit, now and ever and unto ages of ages. Amen.

All holy Trinity, have mercy on us. Lord, cleanse us from our sins. Master, forgive our transgressions. Holy One, look down on us and heal our infirmities to the glory of your name.

Lord, have mercy. Lord, have mercy. Lord, have mercy.

Glory to the Father and to the Son and to the Holy Spirit, now and ever and unto ages of ages. Amen.

Through the prayers of our holy fathers, O Lord Jesus Christ our God, have mercy on us and save us. Amen.

Our Father who are in heaven, hallowed be your name. Your kingdom come, your will be done on earth as it is in heaven. Give us this day our daily bread, and forgive us our trespasses as we forgive those who trespass against us. And lead us not into temptation but deliver us from the evil one.

Through the prayers of our holy fathers, O Lord Jesus Christ our God, have mercy on us and save us. Amen.

Have mercy on us Lord, have mercy on us; we sinners, your servants incapable of response, offer you as Master this supplication: Have mercy on us.

Glory to the Father and to the Son and to the Holy Spirit.

Lord, have mercy on us for we hope in you. Do not be angry with us, do not remember our transgressions but, being merciful, look on us and deliver us from our enemies. For you are our God and we are your people, we are all the work of your hands, and we call your name.

Now and ever and unto ages of ages. Amen.
Open the door of mercy to us, blessed Birth giver of God, so that we who hope in you do not perish but may be saved from adversities through you, for you are the salvation of the Christian race.

Lord, have mercy. *(12 times)*

First Prayer:
To God the Father

By St. Macarius the Great

O eternal God and King of all creation, who have granted me to reach this hour, absolve me of the sins which I have committed during this day in deed, word or thought; and cleanse, O Lord, my humble soul from all stain both physical and spiritual. Grant that I may sleep through this night in peace, O Lord, and arising from my humble bed may I please your all holy name every day of my life and trample underfoot all the enemies, seen and unseen, who wage war against me. Deliver me, Lord from useless thoughts which defile me and from all evil desires. For yours is the kingdom, the power and the glory of the Father and of the Son and of the Holy Spirit, now and ever and unto ages of ages. Amen.

Second Prayer:
To Our Lord Jesus Christ

By St Antioch

O almighty and perfect Word of the Father, Jesus Christ, in your abundant compassion do not separate yourself from me, your servant; instead, ever rest within me, O Jesus the good shepherd of your sheep. Do not give me over to the temptations of the serpent or leave me to the desires of Satan, for the seed of corruption is in me. O Lord God whom we worship, holy King, Jesus Christ, guard me in my sleep with your unwaning light, your Holy Spirit, by whom you granted sanctification to your apostles. Make me worthy and grant me your salvation on my bed, for I am your servant. Shine upon my mind with the light of the understanding of your holy Gospel. Illumine my soul with your Cross, my heart with the purity of your words, my body with your invincible passion. Let me dwell upon your humility, and rouse me in due time to your glory, for you are all glorious, together with your Father who has no beginning and your all holy Spirit, unto all ages. Amen.

Third Prayer:
To the Holy Spirit

O Lord, Heavenly King, Comforter, Spirit of truth, show your compassion to me, your sinful servant; have mercy on me and forgive me, the unworthy one, for all the sins which I have committed against you today as a man, and not only as a man, but even worse than a beast. Forgive all my sins committed willingly or unwillingly, in knowledge or in ignorance, from my youth, from bad habits, from weakness or laziness: If I have sworn by your name or blasphemed it in thought, if I have rebuked anyone or in my anger have spoken ill of another or provoked anyone, if I became angry, or lied, or slept too much, or if a poor man came to me and I did not receive him, if I have provoked by brother or quarreled with him, if I condemned anyone or exalted myself, if I have boasted or lost my temper, or while in prayer my mind turned to vain worldly cares, if I rebelled in thought, or if I have overeaten or drunk too much, if I have laughed foolishly or thought evil, or if I have seen the beauty of another and been wounded by it in my heart, if I have spoken unnecessarily or laughed at my brother's sin while my own sins are countless, if I have neglected to pray, or committed some other sin which I do not remember, for I have done all this and much more. O my Master and Creator, have mercy on me, your lazy and unworthy servant. Loosen, remit, and forgive me, for you are good and the lover of mankind. Thus, miserable, impure, and sinner that I am, I may lie down and sleep in peace, and worship, sing and glorify your all honorable name, together with the Father and his only-begotten Son, now and ever and unto ages of ages. Amen.

Fourth Prayer

O Lord our God, forgive all my sins committed this day in word, deed or thought, for you are good and the lover of mankind. Grant me peaceful and undisturbed sleep. Send me your guardian angel to protect and preserve me from all evil. For you are the guardian of our souls and bodies and we send up glory to you: to the Father and to the Son and to the Holy Spirit, now and ever and unto ages of ages. Amen.

Fifth Prayer

O Lord our God, in whom we believe and whose name we call upon above every name, grant us forgiveness of soul and body as we prepare for sleep. Preserve us from all attacks and dark pleasures, calm the rising of passions, put out the burning of bodily tensions, and grant that we may live in purity in both deed and thought, that in obtaining a life of virtue we may not fall away from your promised blessing, for you are blessed forever. Amen.

Sixth Prayer:
To the Birthgiver of God

O immaculate and blessed Birthgiver of God, Mary, good Mother of the good King, pour forth the mercy of your Son and our God upon my inflamed soul; guide me in virtue by your prayers that I may pass the rest of my life without sin and obtain paradise through you, O Virgin, God's Birthgiver who alone are pure and blessed.

Seventh Prayer:
To the Holy Guardian Angel

O angel of Christ, my holy guardian and protector of my soul and body, forgive all my offences of this day and deliver me from all the evil wiles of the enemy, that I may not move God to anger by a single sin. Pray for me, a sinful and unworthy servant, so that I may be counted worthy of the goodness and mercy of the all holy Trinity and the Mother of my Lord Jesus Christ and all the saints. Amen.

To the Birthgiver of God

O victorious Leader of triumphant hosts, we your servants delivered from all harm sing our grateful thanks, O Birthgiver of God. As you possess invincible might, free us from every calamity that we may cry out to you: Rejoice, O Bride unwedded.

O ever glorious Virgin, Birthgiver of God, Mary, Mother

of Christ our God, accept our prayers and offer them to your Son and our God, that through you he may illumine and save our souls.

All my hope is in you, O Mother of God, keep me under your holy protection.

O Virgin, Birthgiver of God, do not overlook me, a sinner, in need of your help and protection, but have mercy on me for my soul hopes in you.

Prayer to the Holy Trinity

The Father is my hope, the Son is my refuge, the Holy Spirit is my protection. O Holy Trinity glory to you.

It is truly right to call you blessed, O Birthgiver of God. Ever blessed and most pure, and Mother of our God. More honorable than the cherubim, and more glorious beyond compare than the seraphim, who without loss of virginity, gave birth to God the Word. True Birthgiver of God we praise you.

Glory to the Father and to the Son and to the Holy Spirit, now and ever and unto ages of ages. Amen.

Lord, have mercy. Lord, have Mercy. Lord, have mercy.

O Lord Jesus Christ, Son of God, through the prayers of your most pure Mother, of our holy fathers, and of all the saints, have mercy upon me a sinner. Amen.

Prayer

By St. John of Damascus

O Lord, Lover of mankind, is this bed to be my grave, or will you shine upon my wretched soul with the light of day? Behold the grave lies before me and death stands in front of me. I fear your judgement, O Lord, and the eternal torments, but still I do not cease in my evil ways, continually angering you, my Lord God, together with your immaculate Mother, all the heavenly hosts, and my holy guardian angel. I know, O Lord, that I am unworthy of your love for mankind, and that I deserve every condemnation and torment; but I implore you, O Lord, save me according to the abundance of your goodness; for it is no great deed if you grant salvation to the righteous, nor is it a miracle for you to have mercy on those who are pure, for they are deserving of your loving-kindness, but work the wonder of your mercy on me, a sinner, and thus reveal your love for mankind, that my wickedness prevail not over your unspeakable goodness and mercy. Work this deed for me, O Lord, according to your will.

I worship you, all holy and life-creating Trinity, One in essence and undivided: Father, Son and Holy Spirit. I believe, confess, and glorify you. I give thanks to you, praise you, honor you, exalt you, and I pray to you: for your Name's sake, have mercy on me, your unworthy servant. *(three times)*

I venerate you, all holy Birthgiver of God, who by your birthgiving have shown us the true Light. Queen of heaven and earth, hope of those in despair, helper of the weak and reconciler of sinners to God, shelter and protect me from all danger and attacks both of soul and body. I beseech you, help me by your all powerful intercessions.

All holy Lady, Birthgiver of God, accept this humble prayer and present it to your Son and our God that through you, he may illumine and save our souls.

All powers of heaven: Thrones, Dominions, Principalities, Masters, Powers, Cherubim, Seraphim, Archangels and Angels, I pray to you and fall before you, intercede before God for me, a sinner.

Holy and great prophet John, forerunner and baptizer of the Lord, who suffered for Christ and who have boldness before the Master, pray for me a sinner, that I may be saved through your intercessions.

Holy ones of God: apostles, prophets, martyrs, archbishops, those who lived in abstinence, God-fearers, righteous and ascetics, monks, patriarchs, and all saints who suffered for Christ and have boldness before the Master, pray for me a sinner, that I may be saved through your intercessions.

Holy John the golden-mouth, together with Basil the great, Gregory the theologian, Nicholas the wonder-worker, and all the saints who were clothed in the priesthood, help and have mercy on me by your prayers and assistance.

All you holy women: myrrh-bearers, martyrs, God-fearers, and virgins, who served Christ as is due, intercede before God for me, a sinner.

Invincible and divine power of the honorable and life-giving Cross of the Lord do not leave me a sinner, but help me in all danger both of body and soul.

All holy Lady, Birthgiver of God, hope of all Christians, I have no other boldness, no other hope but you, and I beseech you, O my Lady, Birthgiver of God, Mother of Christ my God: Have mercy on me, deliver me from all my wicked ways, and intercede with your compassionate Son and my God that he have mercy on my miserable soul and deliver me from eternal torments, making me worthy of his kingdom.

Illumine my eyes, Christ God, that I may not sleep in death and that the enemy may not say of me: I have conquered him.

Glory to the Father and to the Son and to the Holy Spirit.

Be the support of my soul, O God, for I walk among many snares; deliver me from them and save me, O Good One, as you are the Lover of mankind.

Now and ever and unto ages of ages. Amen.
All glorious Mother of God, holier than the holy angels, we ceaselessly sing to you with our hearts and lips, confessing you as the Birthgiver of God, for indeed you gave birth for us to incarnate God and you ceaselessly pray for our souls.

(Mak the sign of the cross and then you say:)

Let God arise, let his enemies be scattered, let those who hate him flee from before his face. As smoke vanishes, let them vanish; as wax melts before the fire, so let the demons perish before those who love God and sign themselves with the sign of the Cross, saying with joy: Rejoice, most precious and life-giving Cross of the Lord, who cast out demons by the might of him who was crucified upon you, our Lord Jesus Christ, who descended into hades and tramples upon the power of the devil and gave you, his honorable Cross to us, to banish all our enemies. O glorious and life-giving Cross of the Lord, help me together with the holy Lady, Virgin Birthgiver of God and all the saints, unto all ages. Amen.

you, so that together we may bless you all the days of our lives. Amen.

PRAYERS FOR VARIOUS NEEDS

Prayer of One Who is Ill

Lord Jesus Christ our Savior, Physician of souls and bodies, who took on flesh and suffered death on the cross for our salvation, and in your compassionate love cured all kinds of sicknesses and pains, visit me now, O Lord, as I lay suffering, and grant me grace and strength to endure this illness which has stricken me. Grant me patience and acceptance of your will, that I may trust in your loving kindness and tender mercy. I beseech you, bless the means used for my recovery and those who administer them. I know, O Lord, that I deserve any punishment which you may allow me to suffer, for I have offended you and sinned against you in thought, word and deed. Therefore, I humbly pray to you, look upon my weakness and do not deal with me according to my sins, but rather according to your great mercy. Have compassion on me, and let mercy and justice meet, delivering me from this illness and pain. Grant that this sickness may be the means of my repentance and amendment of my life according to your will, that I may spend the rest of my days in your love and fear; that my soul, aided by your grace and sanctified by your Holy Mysteries, may be prepared for its passage to eternal life where, together with all the saints, I may praise and glorify you and the eternal Father and life-giving Spirit. Amen.

Prayer For Women

Almighty Lord, Physician of souls and bodies, who

humble and lift up, who reprimands and again heals, visit [name] with your great mercy, for she is suffering. Stretch forth your arm which is so full of health and healing, and cure her, as You cured Peter's mother-in-law, the woman with an issue of blood, and the daughter of the Canaanite woman, raising her from her bed and pain. Reprove the spirit of weakness which is in her and drive far from her pain, wounds, chills, fever and weakness. If she has sins or transgressions, loosen, remit and forgive them in your infinite love for mankind. O Lord, show Your divine compassion on your creation, in Christ Jesus our Lord, with whom you are blessed, together with Your all holy, good, and life-giving Spirit, now and ever and unto ages of ages. Amen.

Prayer For Men

Almighty Lord, Physician of souls and bodies, who humble and lift up, who reprimands and again heals, visit [name] with your great mercy, for he is suffering. Stretch forth your arm which is so full of health and healing, and cure him, as You cured Cornelius' servant by Your word, the Paralic man by the pool of Bethesda, and the young man who was possessed, raising him from his bed and pain. Reprove the spirit of weakness which is in him and drive far from him pain, wounds, chills, fever and weakness. If he has sins or transgressions, loosen, remit and forgive them in your infinite love for mankind. O Lord, show Your divine compassion on your creation, in Christ Jesus our Lord, with whom you are blessed, together with Your all holy, good, and life-giving Spirit, now and ever and unto ages of ages. Amen.

Prayer of Thanksgiving

Lord Jesus Christ our God, the God of boundless mercies and compassion, whose love for mankind is indescribable and immeasurable, I fall before your glory with fear and trembling as I offer you thanks for all the good things you have granted me, your unworthy servant. I glorify you, praise you and sing to you, the only Lord, Master and Benefactor. Again, falling before you, I offer thanks to your unspeakable compassion and pray that from this day forth, as before, you continue to work your wonders for me, that thus I may grow in love for you and for my neighbor. Deliver me from all evil and need. Grant me peace, and make me worthy, all the days of my life, to offer thanks to you and to cry out and sing to the Father and to the Son and to the Holy Spirit, now and ever and unto ages and ages. Amen.

Prayer For Travellers

Lord Jesus Christ our God, the way, the truth and the life; who travelled together with your servant Joseph, and also with the two disciples as they journeyed to Emmaus; O Master, travel also with me, your servant, and bless my journey. Send a guardian angel with me, as you did with Tobit, to guide and protect me, keeping me unharmed by all danger. In peace, health and good will, may I return home again and glorify your all honored name of the Father and of the Son and of the Holy Spirit, all the days of my life. Amen.

PRAYER BEFORE READING

Holy Scripture

Heavenly King, illumine my mind with the understanding of your Holy Scripture as you helped Your disciples and apostles. Strengthen my will so that I may follow your ordinances to the glory of your holy Name and for the salvation of my soul; for you are the illuminator and savior of our souls. Amen.

Prayer Upon Entering Church

I rejoiced when they said to me: Let us go to the house of the Lord. I enter your house with thanksgiving, O Lord, and worship in your holy temple in fear of you. Guide me, Lord, in your righteousness, direct your path before me, that unhindered, with a pure heart and an upright spirit, I may glorify one Godhead: Father, Son and Holy Spirit. Amen.

Prayer Upon Leaving Church

Lord, my god, I entrust my entire life to you and I pray: Help me, save me and show your loving-kindness to me; grant that I may live wisely, and may the end of my life be Christian, unashamed and peaceful; keep me from all the evils and attacks of the enemy. On your fearful judgment day, show your kindness to me, your servant, and number me among the sheep at your right hand, that together with them I may glorify you unto all ages. Amen.

Prayer at The Beginning of Lent

Hope of all the ends of the world and of those who are far off upon the sea, Lord our God, who long ago in both the old and new law ordained these days of the fast which you have allowed us to reach, we praise you and beseech you: Grant us your strength that we may fulfill these days of abstinence for the glory of your holy Name, the forgiveness of our sins, for the death of passions and for victory over our transgressions. May we be crucified and buried together with you and arise from our deadened sins and thus complete our lives in a manner which is pleasing to you. It is yours to have mercy on us and save us, Christ our god, and we offer glory to you, together with your pre-eternal Father and your all holy and good and life-creating Spirit, now and ever and unto ages of ages. Amen.

Prayer of St. Ephraim

O Lord and Master of my life, remove from me the spirit of laziness, despondency, thirst for power and vain talk. (prostration)

Instead, O Lord and King, grant I may see my own sins and not judge my brother, for you are blessed unto ages of ages. Amen. (prostration)

Lord, have mercy on me, a sinner. *(bow) (3 times)*

Lord, cleanse me, a sinner. *(bow) (3 times)*

You who have created me, save me. *(bow) (3 times)*

Times without number have I sinned against you, forgive me. *(bow) (3 times)*

O Lord and Master of my Life, remove from me the spirit of laziness, despondency, thirst for power and vain talk. Instead, grant me, your servant, the spirit of purity, humility, patience and love. Indeed, O Lord and King, grant that I may see my own sins and not judge my brother, for you are blessed unto ages of ages. Amen. (prostration)

Prayer Before Confession

Hear me, God and Creator, and listen to me, a sinner and your unworthy servant. I have often promised to amend my ways, yet I still remain unchanged. I have sinned, O Lord, I have sinned and I acknowledge my transgressions and am truly repentant. I am ashamed to come before your face, for I have not kept my word to turn from my iniquity. What shall I say for my lack of gratitude, and where shall I turn? I have greatly sinned, my compassionate Master, but I boldly come and fall down at your feet. You accepted to die on the cross because of my wickedness; you call sinners through your holy scriptures, and you cry out in your own voice: Those who come to me shall not be cast out. Therefore, receive me, the unworthy one, O Lord; forgive all my sins, and in your great and immeasurable mercy grant me your grace and your blessings. I am truly sorry for all in which I have transgressed and angered your goodness by word, deed or thought, willingly or unwillingly. I promise that from this day forward, with your grace and help, I shall not return to my former ways, for it is better to die than to transgress one of your commandments. I resolve to obey you now and forever, and to worship your all-holy name, O my sweet Jesus, and to confess you to the ages of ages. Amen.

Go to confession with a contrite heart willing to transform your life and renounce sin.

Preparation For Holy Communion

Preparing yourself to partake of the divine Body and Blood of Christ is of the utmost importance. Hence, on the evening prior to receiving Holy Communion, the following prayers are said.

Through the prayers of our holy fathers, O Lord Jesus Christ our God, have mercy on us and save us. Amen.

Glory to you, O God, glory to you.

Heavenly King, Comforter, Spirit of truth, who are present everywhere and fulfilling all things; Treasury of blessings and Source of life, come abide in us, cleanse us of all stain, and save our souls, O Good One.

Holy God, Holy Mighty, Holy Immortal, have mercy on us. Holy God, Holy Mighty, Holy Immortal, have mercy on us.

Glory to the Father and to the Son and to the Holy Spirit, now and ever unto ages of ages. Amen.

All holy Trinity, have mercy on us. Lord, cleanse us of our sins. Master, forgive our transgressions. Holy One, look down on us and heal our infirmities to the glory of your name.

Lord, have mercy. Lord, have mercy. Lord, have mercy.

Glory to the Father and to the Son and to the Holy Spirit, now and ever unto ages of ages. Amen.

Our Father who are in heaven, hallowed be your name. Your kingdom come, your will be done on earth as it is in heaven. Give us this day our daily bread, and forgive us our trespasses as we forgive those who trespass against us. And lead us not into temptation, but deliver us from the evil one.

Through the prayers of our holy fathers, O Lord Jesus Christ our God, have mercy on us and save us. Amen.

Lord, have mercy. *(12 times)*

Come, let us worship God our King. Come, let us worship and bow down before Christ our King. Come, let us worship and bow down before Christ himself, our God and King.

Psalm 51

Have mercy on me, O God, in your goodness, in your great tenderness wipe away my faults; wash me clean of my guilt, purify me from my sin. For I am well aware of my faults, I have my sin constantly in mind, having sinned against none other than you, having done what you regard as wrong. You are just when you pass sentence on me, blameless when you give judgment. You know I was born guilty, a sinner from the moment of conception. Yet, since you love sincerity of heart, teach me the secrets of wisdom. Purify me with hyssop until I am clean; wash me until I am whiter than snow. Instill some joy and gladness into me, let the bones you have crushed rejoice again Hide your face from my sins, wipe out all my guilt. God, create a clean heart in me, put into me a new and constant spirit, do not banish me from your presence, do not deprive me of your Holy Spirit. Be my savior again, renew my joy, keep my spirit steady and willing; and I shall teach transgressors the way to you, and to you the sinners will return. Save me from death, God my savior and my tongue will acclaim your righteousness; Lord, open my lips and my mouth will speak out your praise. Sacrifice gives you no pleasure, were I to offer holocaust, you would not have it. My sacrifice is this broken spirit, you will not scorn this crushed and broken heart. Show your favor graciously to Zion, rebuild the walls of Jerusalem. Then there will be proper sacrifice to please you - holocaust and whole oblation - and young bulls to be offered on your altar.

First Prayer

By St. Basil the Great

Master, Lord, Jesus Christ our God, fount of life and immortality, creator of all things both visible and invisible, Son of the eternal Father, who together with him are eternal and without beginning; who in your goodness, in these latter days, bore flesh and were crucified, sacrificing yourself for us ungrateful and thankless ones; who through your Blood have renewed our nature which was destroyed by sin; O Immortal King, also receive my repentance, for I am a sinner. Look upon me and hear my voice; I have sinned, O Lord, I have sinned against heaven and before you, and I am unworthy to look upon the height of your glory. I have offended your goodness by trampling upon your precepts and ignoring your commandments. But, Lord, who bear malice toward none, who are long-suffering and all merciful; you have not let me perish in my transgressions, but you await my complete return. Lover of mankind, you said through your prophet: I do not desire the death of a sinner, but rather that he turn and live. O Master, you do not desire that the work of your hands should perish, nor do you await the fall of mankind, "but you desire that all be saved in the true knowledge which is to come." Although I have completely subjected myself to sin and am unworthy of heaven, of earth and of this passing life; even though I am a slave to delights and have disgraced your image, yet I still do not lose hope in salvation, wretched as I am, for you have made and fashioned me. I place my hope in your boundless mercy and approach you: Receive me, O harlot and the thief, the publican and the prodigal son. Remove the heavy burden of my sins, for you take away the sin of the world and heal man's weaknesses; you call the weary and over-burdened, giving them rest; you came to call the sinners, not the just, to repentance; thus cleanse me of all impurity, both of soul and body. Teach me to practice holiness in the fear of you, that with a clear conscience I may partake of a share of your holy Mysteries and be united with your holy Body and Blood; thus, together with the Father and the Spirit, you may dwell and stay in me Lord Jesus Christ, my God, may my partaking of you pure and life-creating Mysteries not be for condemnation, nor for weakness of body or soul, for I partake of them unworthily; but to my last breath, grant that I may receive a portion of your holy Mysteries without condemnation, for the communion of the Holy Spirit, as food for eternal life and for an acceptable response at your fearful judgment seat. Together with your chosen ones, may I participate in your unfading goodness which you have prepared for those who love you, O Lord, glorified to the ages of ages. Amen.

Second Prayer

Lord my God, I know that I am neither worthy nor prepared for you to enter under the roof of my soul's dwelling, for it is all deserted and in ruins and you cannot find a place fitting to lay your head in me. But as you bowed down and descended from the heights, so now bow down to my humility. As you condescended to lay in a cave, in a manger of speechless animals, thus condescend to enter my defiled body. Just as you did not consider Simon the leper as unworthy, but rather entered his house and dined with sinners, so deign also to enter the meek, leprous and sinful dwelling of my soul. And as you did not despise the sinful woman who came and touched you, thus be merciful to me as I come and touch you, for I am a sinner like her. Just as you did not recoil from her defiled and unclean lips which kissed you, so do not recoil from my defiled and unclean mouth, nor my unclean and profane lips, nor my sordid tongue. But let the burning coal of your immaculate Body and precious Blood be for my sanctification and illumination, for the healing of my humble soul and body, for alleviation of the weight of my numerous sins, as a guard against diabolic works, for the estrangement and elimination of my evil and wicked ways, for the death of passions, for fulfillment of your commandments, advancement in your divine grace and attainment of your kingdom. I do not approach you carelessly, Christ God; rather, I come trusting in your unspeakable goodness so that I may not remain a stranger to communion with you, and be ensnared by the cunning wolf. I therefore pray to you, only Holy One and Master: Sanctify my soul and body, my mind and hear, to the depths of my being, renew me and plant the fear of you deep inside me and immutably instill your holiness in me. May it be for my help and assistance, guiding my life in peace, and grant that I may stand at your right hand together with the saints; through the prayers and intercessions of your all-pure Mother, of the bodiless angels, the immaculate powers and all the saints who have been pleasing to you throughout the ages. Amen.

Third Prayer

By St. Simeon the Translator

Only pure and spotless Lord, who in your unspeakable mercy and love for mankind took on our whole nature from the pure and virgin blood of her who ineffably gave birth to you through the coming of the divine Spirit and the will of the eternal Father; Lord Jesus Christ, the wisdom, peace and power of God, who bodily suffered the life-giving and saving Passion: the cross, the nails, the spear and death, put to death the bodily passions which devastate my soul. As through your burial you plundered the kingdom of hades, so bury my wicked intentions and scatter the evil spirits through good thoughts. Through your life-giving resurrection on the third day, you raised our fallen ancestor; also raise me who have fallen in sin, and instill an image of repentance in me. Through your glorious ascension to heaven you deified the body which you had assumed and honored it by placing it at the right of the Father, grant me also to partake of your holy Mysteries so that I too may find a place at the right of those who are saved. Through the descent of the comforting Spirit you molded your disciples as chosen vessels, so present me also as a dwelling of his coming. And just as you will come again to judge the whole world in righteousness, grant that I may also meet you, my judge and creator, on the clouds together with all the saints who unceasingly praise and glorify you, together with your Father without beginning and your all holy good and life-creating Spirit, now and ever and unto ages of ages. Amen.

Fourth Prayer

By St. Simeon the Translator

Just as I will stand one day before your fearful and undissembling judgment seat, Christ God, answering the questions regarding the evils I have committed, so I stand now, before the coming of my day of judgment, before you and your fearful and holy angels at your holy altar. My conscience impells me to lay forth my evil deeds and transgressions and to expose them openly. Lord, look upon my lowliness and forgive all my sins; you can see that my transgressions have multiplied more than the hairs on my head. What evil have I not committed? What sinful thing have I not done? What form of wickedness have I not imagined in my soul? You know that I have gone beyond the bounds of depravity in my deeds and have been proud, arrogant, contemptuous, blasphemous, spoken idly, laughed uncontrollably, been drunken, gluttonous, eaten beyond measure, been malicious, envious, loved money and possessions, extorted others, loved myself, sought glory, been grasping, unjust, shameful, covetous, spoken evilly and transgressed. I have stained and defiled all my senses down to the depth of my being, and have done nothing worthwhile. I have become an absolute dwelling of the devil. Lord, I know that my transgressions have mounted higher than my head, but the greatness of your compassion is incomparable and the mercy of your bounty is free of spite and indescribable. There is no sin which surpasses your love for mankind. Therefore, wondrous King and all gracious Lord, show your wondrous mercy to me a sinner; show me the power of your goodness; show me the strength of your long-suffering mercy and receive me a sinner as I turn to you. Receive me as you received the prodigal son, the thief, and the harlot. Receive me who have sinned against you immeasurably in word and in deed, with unrestrained appetite and unseemly behavior. Just as you received those who had done nothing worthy and came to you at the eleventh hour, so also receive me, a sinner; for I have sinned greatly and defiled myself. I have provoked your Holy Spirit and infuriated your mercy, O Lover of mankind, in deed, word and thought, at night and day, openly and secretly, willingly and unwillingly. I know that you will ask me of those things in which I knowingly and unforgivably have sinned. But, Lord, do not pass your just judgment on me; do not reproach me in your anger nor punish me in your rage. Be merciful to me, Lord, for I am not only weak, but I am also your creation. Lord, though you have instilled the fear of you in me, still I have done wrong in your sight. I have sinned against none other than you; but I beseech you: Do not put your servant on trial, for if you never overlooked our sins, Lord, Lord, who could survive? I have reached the very depths of sin and am not worthy nor able to look and gaze upon the heights of heaven because of the multitude of my innumerable sins. Every evil work, imagination, and diabolic scheme, all the wickedness of hades which leads to sin, physical delights and other innumerable passions have all found a place in me. What form of sin has not defiled me? By what evil have I not been ensnared? I have committed every sin and have allowed all unforgivable pleasures to enter my soul. I have made myself worthless before God and before man. I have fallen to such a depth of evil sin; who will raise me up again? Lord, my God, I place my hope in you. If there still exists a hope of salvation for me, then let your love for mankind overcome the multitude of my transgressions. Be my savior, and in your goodness and mercy loosen, forgive and remit all in which I have sinned against you; for my soul has been filled with many evils and there is no hope for salvation in me. Have mercy on me, O God, in your goodness and do not punish me as my sins deserve, but turn to me, be my support, deliver my soul from the evils which have grown inside it and from all which has accumulated in it. Have mercy on me, in your goodness, for wherever sin has been multiplied, may there also be the abundance of your grace. Thus I will praise and glorify you all the days of my life. For you are the God of those who sin and the Savior of those who do wrong and to you is due glory, together with your eternal Father and your all holy good and life-creating Spirit, now and ever and unto ages of ages. Amen.

Fifth Prayer

By St. John of Damascus

O Lord, Master, Jesus Christ our God, who alone

have authority to forgive man's sins; as you are good and the lover of mankind, overlook all my transgressions committed knowingly or unknowingly, and grant that I may partake uncondemned of your divine, glorious, pure and life-creating Mysteries. May this communion not be for condemnation, nor for the increase of sin, but for cleansing, sanctification and obtaining of the life and kingdom which is to come; as a defense, help and banishment of those who fight against me and to the elimination of my many iniquities; for you are the God of mercy and compassion and the lover of mankind and to you is due all glory, together with the Father and the Holy Spirit, now and ever and unto ages of ages. Amen.

Sixth Prayer

By St. Basil the Great

I know, Lord, that if I unworthily commune of your most pure Body and your precious Blood, I am blameworthy, and I eat and drink judgment on myself for not discerning your Body and Blood, O Christ, my God. But encouraged by your compassion, I approach you who said: Whoever eats my Flesh and drinks my Blood dwells continually in me and I dwell in him. Therefore, be merciful, O Lord, and do not punish me, a sinner, but deal with me according to your mercy. May your holy Mysteries be for healing and cleansing, for enlightenment and protection, for salvation and hallowing of soul and body and for the dispersion of every illusion, evil deed and diabolic work directed against me. May they be for boldness and love towards you, for correction and constancy of life, for growth in virtue and perfection, for fulfillment of your commandments and communion with the Holy Spirit. And may they be food for that life to come and a good response before your dread judgment seat, but not for judgment nor condemnation.

Seventh Prayer

By St. Simeon the New Theologian

O my Christ, receive my prayer which comes forth from vile lips, from a profane heart, from an impure tongue and a soiled soul; and do not turn aside from my words, nor my habits, nor my shamelessness, but bestow confidence in me that I may say that which I desire, O my Christ; or rather, show me exactly what I should do and say. I have sinned more than the sinful woman who, when she found where you were staying, purchased myrrh and daringly approached you and anointed your feet, my Master, Christ and God. She approached you wholeheartedly and you did not reject her, so also do not turn aside from me, O Word, but let me touch and kiss your feet, daring to anoint them with a fount of tears as with precious myrrh. Cleanse me, O Word, and wash me in my tears. Forgive my trespasses and guide my life. You know my many errors, you know my sores and you behold my wounds; but you also know my faith, you behold my will and you hear my sighs. Nothing is hidden from you, Lord, my God, my creator and deliverer; not a teardrop nor even part of a drop. Your eyes know even those things which I have not yet done are already written in your book. Look upon my humility; look upon the depth of my fatigue and forgive all my sins, O God of all. Thus, with a clean heart, fearful conscience and humble soul, may I partake of your immaculate and holy Mysteries through which you deify and give life to those who eat and drink of them with a pure heart. You have said, my Master: Whoever eats my Body and drinks my Blood lives in me and I in him. How true are those words, my Master and God! For he who partakes of the divine and deifying Gifts is not alone, but with you, my Christ, who came from the thrice-radiant Light which enlightens the world. Therefore, tearfully and with humility of soul, I approach you, as you see, so that I may not stay alone, without you, the giver of life, my breath, my life, my joy, the salvation of the world. I beg that I may be delivered from my sins and may partake uncondemned of your life-giving and spotless Mysteries. May you remain with me, the thrice-wretched one, as you foretold, so that the sly deceiver may not ravage me upon finding me absent from your grace, and, being thus deceived, carry me away from your deifying words. I therefore fall before you and fervently cry: Just as you accepted the prodigal son and the sinful woman when they came to you, so also receive me, sinful and defiled, as I now draw near to you in humility of soul, O merciful One. I know, O Savior, that no one else has sinned against you or committed such deeds as I have; but I also know that the greatness of my trespasses and the multitude of my sins do not surpass the great patience of my God nor his sublime love for mankind. But in your everlasting compassion, you cleanse, you illumine, and unite to the light him who fervently repents, that he may partake, without envy, of your divinity. You speak to him as to your true friend of those things which are beyond reach to the minds of angels and men. These things give me courage, they give me wings, my Christ, and I place my hope in the abundance of your grace to us and, rejoicing and trembling, I partake of the fire though I am dry grass, and O-wonder! - I am refreshed and unburnt, as the bush of long ago which was in flames but not consumed. Therefore, thankful in mind, heart and to the depths of my soul and body, I bow before you in worship and glorify you, my God, who are truly blessed now and in all ages. Amen.

Eighth Prayer

By St. John Chrysostom

Lord, loosen, remit, forgive all the sins which I have committed against you in word, deed or thought, willingly or unwillingly, in knowledge or ignorance; forgive them all, as you are good and love mankind. Through the prayers of your most pure Mother, of your ministering angels, the holy powers and all the saints who have pleased you throughout the ages; grant that uncondemned I may receive your most pure Body and precious Blood for the healing of soul and body and the cleansing of my wicked thoughts. For yours is the kingdom and the power and the glory of the Father and of the Son and of the Holy Spirit, now and ever and unto ages of ages. Amen.

Ninth Prayer

By St. John Chrysostom

I am not worthy, O Lord and Master, to have you enter beneath the roof of my soul; but since you, the lover of mankind, wish to dwell in me, I boldly approach. Command me, and I shall open the doors which you yourself have made; that in your constant love for mankind you may enter therein and enlighten my darkened mind. I believe that you will do this, for you did not send away the harlot who came to you in tears; you did not refuse the thief who acknowledged your kingdom, nor did you leave the penitent persecutor, Paul, to continue in his ways. Rather, you numbered among your friends all those who came to you in penitence, for you alone are blessed always, now and to ages unending. Amen.

Tenth Prayer

By St. John Chrysostom

Lord Jesus Christ, my God, loosen, remit, have mercy on me and forgive me a sinner, your worthless and unworthy servant who has fallen into sin. Forgive my ignorance and all the trespasses which I have committed against you from my youth to this day and hour, knowingly or unknowingly, in word, in deed, in thought or mind, by habit or with complete awareness. Through the intercessions of her who without stain gave you birth, the pure and ever-virgin Mary, your Mother, my only invincible hope and protection and deliverer; grant me to partake uncondemned of your immaculate, immortal, life-creating and fearful Mysteries, for the forgiveness of sins, for eternal life, for sanctification, illumination, fortification, curing and health of soul and body and for the erasing and perdition of all my thought, intentions, evil habits and nightmares of the dark and evil spirits. For yours is the kingdom, the power, glory, honor and worship, together with the Father and the Holy Spirit

now and ever and unto ages of ages. Amen.

Eleventh Prayer

By St. John of Damascus

I stand before the doors of your house and still do not put aside evil thoughts. But, O Christ God, who reformed the publican and had mercy on the Canaanite woman and opened the doors of paradise to the thief, also open to me your great love for mankind, and receive me who come and touch you as did the harlot and the woman who suffered from hemorrhage. For she was immediately healed by touching the he, of your robe and the other obtained forgiveness of her sins by embracing your pure feet. And I, a wretched one, dare to presume to receive your whole Body; and thus, lest I am burned, receive me as you received those who were penitent, and enlighten my spiritual senses, burning only the iniquity of my sins. Through the intercessions of her who without seed bore you, and through the heavenly powers, for you are blessed for ever. Amen.

Twelfth Prayer

By St. John Chrysostom

I believe, O Lord, and I confess that you are truly the Christ, the Son of the living God who came into the world to save sinners, among whom I am first. I also believe that this is your own pure Body and this is your own precious Blood. Therefore I pray to you: have mercy on me and forgive my voluntary and involuntary trespasses, in word and in deed, in knowledge and in ignorance. Make me worthy, without condemnation, to partake of your most pure Mysteries for forgiveness of sins and for everlasting life. Amen.

PRAYERS OF THANKSGIVING

After Holy Communion

After partaking of the divine and life-giving Gifts, offer praise and thanksgiving to God:

Glory to you, O Lord! Glory to you, O Lord! Glory to you, O God!

Prayer of St. Basil

I thank you, Lord my God, that you have not rejected me, a sinner, but have counted me, the unworthy, worthy to partake of your most Gifts. But, O Master, Lover of mankind, who died for us and arose and bestowed on us these fearsome and life-creating Mysteries for the good and sanctification of our souls and bodies; grant that they may be to me for healing of soul and body, for repelling of every assault of the adversary, for illumination of the eyes of my heart, for peace of my spiritual powers, for unconquerable faith, for unfeigned love, for perfection of wisdom, for observing your commandments, for increase of your divine grace, and attainment of your kingdom. For preserved by them your holiness, may I ever remember your grace and live not for myself, but for you, our master and benefactor. Thus passing through this life with the hope of unending life, may I attain everlasting rest, where the voice of those who praise is unceasing and the sweetness of those who behold the unspeakable beauty of your face is without end. For you are the true desire and the unspeakable joy of those who love you, Christ our God, and all creation praises you forever. Amen.

Second Prayer of St. Basil

Master, Christ God, King of the ages and Creator of all, I thank you for all the good things you have given me and for the communion of your most pure and life-creating Mysteries. Therefore, I pray to you, O good One, Lover of mankind, preserve me under your shelter and under the shadow of your wings. Grant me, to my last breath, to worthily partake with a pure conscience of your holy Mysteries for forgiveness of sins and for life everlasting. For you are the bread of life, the fountain of holiness, the giver of all good and we offer glory to you, together with the Father and the Holy Spirit, now and ever and unto ages of ages. Amen.

Prayer of St. Simeon

Graciously have you given me your body for nourishment, you, who are a fire consuming the unworthy. Burn me not, my Creator, but instead enter into my members, my veins, my heart and burn the thorns of all my sins. Cleanse my soul, sanctify my mind and bones. Illumine my five senses, fill me with fear of you and ever shelter, help and preserve me from soul-destroying words and deeds. Cleanse me, purify me, guide me and enlighten me. Because of holy Communion, show me to be only a dwelling of your Spirit and not a shelter for sin. May every evil work, all passion, flee from me as from fire. I offer you as intercessors all the saints: the leaders of the bodiless powers, your forerunner, the wise apostles and together with them, your most honorable and pure Mother. Receive their intercessions, O my merciful Christ and make me, your servant, a child of light. For you are the sanctification and illumination of our souls, O good One, and to you, as is right, as God and Master, we offer glory day by day.

Prayer of St. Cyril of Alexandria

May your holy Body be to me for eternal life and your precious Blood for forgiveness of sins, O Lord Jesus Christ our God. May this Eucharist be to me for joy, health and gladness; and at your second and awesome coming, count, a sinner, worthy to stand at the right of your glory. Through the intercessions of your most pure Mother and of all your saints. Amen.

Prayer of St. Simeon

Now Master, you can let your servant go in peace, just as you promised; because my eyes have seen the salvation which you have prepared for all the nations to see, a light to enlighten the pagans and the glory of your people Israel.

Holy God, Holy Mighty, Holy Immortal, have mercy on us. Holy God, Holy Mighty, Holy Immortal, have mercy on us. Holy God, Holy Mighty, Holy Immortal, have mercy on us.

Glory to the Father and to the Son and to the Holy Spirit,

now and ever unto ages of ages. Amen.

All holy Trinity, have mercy on us. Lord, cleanse us of our sins. Master, forgive our transgressions. Holy One, look down on us and heal our infirmities to the glory of your name.

Lord, have mercy. Lord, have mercy. Lord, have mercy.

Glory to the Father and to the Son and to the Holy Spirit, now and ever unto ages of ages. Amen.

Our Father, who are in heaven, hallowed be your name. Your kingdom come, your will be done on earth as it is in heaven. Give us this day our daily bread, and forgive us our trespasses as we forgive those who trespass against us. And lead us not into temptation, but deliver us from the evil one.

Through the prayers of our holy fathers, O Lord Jesus Christ our God, have mercy on us and save us. Amen

If the Divine Liturgy of St. John Chrysostom was served, the following hymns are read:

Glory to the Father and to the Son and to the Holy Spirit.

You received divine grace from heaven, O most worthy one, and by your lips you teach all to worship one God in Trinity. Therefore it is right to praise you, O John the Golden-mouth, for you are a teacher revealing things divine.

Now and ever and unto ages of ages. Amen.

Invincible guardian of Christians, constant mediator before the Creator, disregard not the voice of supplication of sinners, but, O good one, speedily help us who in faith cry out to you: Quickly intercede and hasten to supplicate, ever guarding those who honor you, O Birthgiver of God.

If the Divine Liturgy of St. Basil was served, the following hymns are read:

Your renown has spread throughout the world which received the divinely inspired words of your teachings. You revealed the true nature of created things, and brought order to the lives of men. Holy father and royal priest Basil, pray to Christ God that he may save our souls.

Glory to the Father and to the Son and to the Holy Spirit.

You are clearly a firm foundation of the Church for you bestowed everlasting domination to mankind, sealing it by your teachings, O holy father Basil, announcer of things divine.

Now and ever and unto ages of ages. Amen.
O invincible guardian of Christians… (see above)

If the Divine Liturgy of the Pre-Sanctified Gifts was served, the following hymns are read:

Glorious Gregory, who received divine grace from God on high and are strengthened by his power, you willingly followed the Holy Gospel of Christ and were rewarded by him for your efforts, O blessed one. Intercede with him that he save our souls.

Glory to the Father and to the Son and to the Holy Spirit.

You proved yourself as a shepherd, following the example of Christ, the first of shepherds. You guided monks into the heavenly sheepfold, teaching them the commandments of Christ, and you now rejoice with them in the heavenly tabernacles.

Now and ever unto ages of ages. Amen.

O invincible guardian of Christians... (see above)

Lord, have mercy. *(12 times)*

More honorable than the cherubim, and more glorious beyond compare than the seraphim, who without loss of virginity gave birth to God the Word, true Birthgiver of God, we praise you.

Glory to the Father and to the Son and to the Holy Spirit, now and ever and unto ages of ages. Amen.

Lord, have mercy. Lord, have mercy. Lord, have mercy.

Through the prayers of our holy fathers, O Lord Jesus Christ our God, have mercy on us and save us. Amen.

Glory be to God for all things!

www.ingramcontent.com/pod-product-compliance
Lightning Source LLC
Chambersburg PA
CBHW061513040426
42450CB00008B/1589